WE ARE COMPLETE!

A book by
Isabel Hernandez

Contents

THE STORY BEGINS HERE..........

Introduction.

This is the story of a soul, existing in perfect harmony among a group of similar beings, in a higher dimension. An enlightened being, a being who lives outside of space and time. The soul would split itself and be divided into multiple parts in order to accomplish its mission on earth.

The story begins when the entity is in complete awareness, a perfect example of self in its full unity and glory. The enlightened being will describe the journey ahead and what will happen as direct experience for the other part that is sent to earth, the connection between both parts, and how each part plays a fundamental role for the growth and expansion of self.

The entity divides itself into two parts. One part that goes to earth, and the bigger part that stays between dimensions. The part that stays between dimensions is not affected by time and lives in completion and awareness of all. The enlightened being patiently awaits the awakening of the part that was sent to earth, but it also plays an active role by guiding and helping the other part which we call *the incarnated soul.*

While walking the path of enlightenment, the incarnated soul will narrate her story of discovering her mission on earth. While experiencing life, it will encounter *interventions* from the part that stays out of time. During its journey the incarnated soul will make discoveries, get inspired, feel the calling of something bigger than itself, and awaken realizations of awareness. Every realization will be one step closer to self-awareness. When the journey on earth is done, both parts will once again unite.

AND THEN SHE WAS THERE

And then she was there, sitting on the old mattress she had for a bed, resting her back against the brick wall. The room was full of silence with only an old stove, a table with a few chairs and an old petroleum heater to keep her warm. She was young- barely sixteen, with long breaded hair, wearing a loose dress. She looked sad and lost, looking out at empty space, while rubbing her pregnant belly, she seemed afraid of her future.

This was the first time I saw my mother, while I was still in her womb!

REINCARNATION .... WHO KNOWS HOW MANY.

My name is Isabel. I was born in Juarez Mexico, the oldest of eight siblings. I grew up in very poor conditions, subjected to the moods and violent outbreaks of an alcoholic father and a weak, submissive mother. My father hated my existence from the beginning because I was the reason he felt forced to marry my mother, a woman he never loved.

In his eyes, my mother was unworthy because she had a child "out of wedlock" prior to meeting him. In order for my mother to be with him, she had given the child to her mother to raise.

My childhood was an eternal torment with a long agony that marked my soul for the rest of my existence.

Suppressed memories still pup up to remind me of the condition I left behind. Memories like the following that I'll like to share with you.

When I was around 7 years old with a younger sister and brother my parents used to send us out of the one-bedroom house. They kept us outside for hours. We were hungry and tired sitting outside on hot summer days, waiting for them to let us back in, but they didn't seem to care. Hours later we usually heard them screaming and throwing things at each other, followed by my father beating my mother.

One of those times, when he opened the door for us to get in, the air smelled thick-a smell that I didn't recognize until much later in life as a combination of alcohol and sex- and I saw my mother laying on the floor unconscious.

I ran to hold her hand. *Had my father killed her this time?* My siblings and I were screaming and crying on the floor around our mother, thinking she was surely dead. On any other day I would have been afraid of my father, but on this specific day I experienced a feeling I never had before: I experienced hate towards him. I looked at him with hate in my eyes, while he drunkenly walked around in circles, while yelling at us to be quiet, repeating over and over "You don't know how unworthy your mother is."

Tired of listening I stood up and yelled at him, "Look at what you have done, you killed our mother and I hate you for that!"

My father looked at me for two seconds surprised by my reaction, and without saying one more word took his truck keys and left the house. Fortunately one of the neighbors heard the commotion and came to help us. She gave something to my mom to wake her up, and told us that she would be ok.

On another occasion, my father took us to grandma's house. I remember that day vividly. The women gathered in the kitchen, while the men sat on the couch talking. All the kids were outside playing. I came back inside, hearing my father saying to his brother "Watch this," as I ran by the couch where he was sitting, he stuck out his leg to make me trip, and I did.

I cut the skin on my knee and started crying, "Get up!" my father said cursing at me. I looked at my mother, she saw what he did, but was too afraid to say anything. My father and his brother were laughing at me.

Episodes like these happened often during all of my childhood. There were days when I secretly wished my father would die in an accident, so he wouldn't come back home drunk to mistreat us.

I never understood why my mom didn't stand up for herself, or for us. Maybe she felt alone, or maybe she was too afraid. Many times I saw her lost, staring into empty space, which usually happened after one of the big fights. At different times I had ask my mother "Why don't you leave dad, I can take care of the children while you work." she always replied " You don't understand, it's not that easy, go and take care of your chores." It made me sad that I couldn't help her with any advise. I was only a child trying to understand her *grownup world*, and why she never had the courage to confront him, even when it affected her own children.

She was not allowed to go to any of my school activities, meetings or even my graduations. The only place she was allowed to go was to the market place, to get groceries. Many times, I had to go by myself. Other times a neighbor, a sweet lady that sometimes took care of us children, or my grandmother would accompany me.

However, as I started to grow older, my courage grew with me. One afternoon, coming back from school, I found my parents in the middle of an argument that, as usual, turned into a physical fight.

For one moment, I asked myself "how long do I have to deal with this?" My mother was facing my father, holding a pair of scissors in front of her, threatening him to stay away, while he, drunk as usual was ready to hit her in the face. Without hesitation, I dropped my books and not knowing how, blocked my father's fist in mid air.

Surprised by my reaction, my father looked at me and said "what are you doing?" Driven by anger, I faced him and replied "this is the last time you raise your hand against my mother". Sarcastically he smirked, "or what? are you going to fight me?" Not backing down, I answered firmly "I'm not afraid of you, I will call the police and do anything to stop you." Turning towards the door, my father said "we'll see about that," then he left in his truck.

The adrenaline that had given me the necessary courage to physically confront him, suddenly left my body, leaving my legs shaking. I did not know what would happen next, would he come back to *kill me* or would my actions even change anything. Regardless, being tired of their fights, I had to do something.

Their arguments off course continued, but after that day he never again raised his hand against my mother, or at least not in front of me.

What I could never understand was why my father was attentive to my siblings, but not to me.

I was constantly tired because of the multiple chores I had to tend to since my mother was pregnant every other year. My only escape was going to school, walking a few miles each way and spending a few hours away from the chaos I was living in. On the way back, my stomach always hurt just thinking about what I would find when I got home. Growing up, all of those details used to matter to me when I tried to understand the reasons of my misfortune. They mattered to me when I tried to understand what I did wrong to get punished with so much cruelty. It mattered when I tried to understand my karma. But I was incapable of understanding my own misfortune and why things turned out the way they were, or what I did wrong before being born.

In trying to understand the reasons for why some people suffer and why others have it easier, I lost myself trying to understand *God's mind* and what *His plan* was for me. Kind of like a monkey looking into a mirror, not knowing what is in front of it. It became a reality I wanted to suppress. Too many questions with no real answers!

I always felt that none of what we see as *reality*, is real. I always felt that something was missing, something that I couldn't see. Nothing made sense, but I tried to act as if it did.

I experienced strange phenomena like revelations, intuition and dreams, but I was never comfortable sharing those experiences with other people, they seemed not to understand, or be prompt to judge as *crazy*, so I suppressed my abilities.

For so long I felt as if I didn't belong in this place, no matter what place that was. The problem was that I didn't know where I belonged. I served myself with self pity, hoping that someday, somebody would come to show me the way, but no one did. I was always looking for something, not knowing what.

Many times I thought, *maybe I'm just not important enough*

to be saved, or maybe I was into the wrong religion.
Because of that, I looked into different religions and
philosophies. They all felt empty to me, so I thought that
there was something wrong with me.

I became angry and disappointed with the world and
myself. Later in life, I realized that there's no need to blame
the world for what I was taught, because one way or
another everybody was taught the same or similar.

However, every time I tried following somebody else's
dogma, I always felt a weird feeling of self-betrayal. It felt
as if I was looking in the wrong place, but I didn't know
where else to look.

So I tried to ignore that feeling and cover it up with
something else, while inside I was full of fears and doubts.
Nonetheless, I was always fascinated with the study of the
brain/mind and its mysteries. Later on in college I even
took multiple courses of psychology. However, none of
what was in the curriculum made any sense to what I was
experiencing. I thought, *how am I going to get a handle on
the study of the mind when I disagree with what is taught?*
Again, I felt as if science was missing a very big and
important piece of knowledge and information.

By then, I didn't know where else to search. I was
disappointed by religion and science. To me they felt
incomplete, so I felt lost!

One day I finally realized that my questions could only be
answered by me. I realized that the person I needed to get
to know was the one inside. I needed to learn how to listen
to the voice in my heart, but I did not know how, since that
was precisely the part I always tried to push aside. I had
suppressed my intuition, my dreams, thinking they would
go away if I ignored them. By then, I realized that I owed
myself much more than I ever thought I did.

Things started to become clearer to me after I realized that
my own life is a mystery. A mystery only I could unravel.
My questions started to be answered one by one, when I

learned to connect with the "God" within me. Life would continue to unfold piece by piece like a big puzzle as I ventured further into this human existence.

One important thing that helped me to understand my situation was the realization that time is not linear as we are taught to think; it is more like a body of water where there is no beginning or end and everything is interconnected with everything else.

Let me give you another example.
When I was a child, I used to live in fear of many things. I was very fragile. I remember having nightmares even as an infant.
I used to wake up crying many times. My mother didn't know what scared me so much or why I continued to have repeated nightmares. Later, when I was able to talk, I told her about the nightmare I kept having over and over. In this nightmare, I was four or five years old and in a room with my mother, when an old woman with a little evil creature came to the house and entered under false pretenses.
The woman chased us around the room and tried to inject me with a big syringe, while my mother was trying to protect me from her. To me, that woman looked like an old witch with her little evil friend.
My mother was very surprised to hear that from me, and when I got older and able to understand the meaning, she told me that during her pregnancy, my grandmother, a nurse, tried to give her something to induce an abortion.

How could I possibly know what happened to my mother when she was still pregnant with me, and how was it possible to carry a trauma from the womb, when the fetus was not completely developed as a baby? How could it be possible to carry the memory of seeing my mother pregnant with me? Was I observing myself from an astral body before I even had a physical one and for some reason was able to remember the experience? Or was I observing from a different point in time?

That's when I realized we have more than five senses. These experiences became a fascinating subject to study and a way to try to understand my own situation.

There is so much we do not know about the mysteries of life, what we are made of and how everything connects to everything else.

Why do we choose certain experiences, our parents, siblings, friends or enemies? Why do we choose our lovers, our pets, our tendencies, weaknesses, talents and strengths? Why do we choose different demographics, skin color or social standings? Does any of this make any sense?

No, it doesn't, because we were trained from childhood not to question those things and to believe that *God* created us equal and we're all the same in *his eyes*. Yet in the eyes of humans we are born under different conditions and taught to completely ignore our senses. I was taught to believe in a God that is a jealous and vengeance God, one we must obey and fear! What kind of teaching is that?

I believe we were taught wrong, so we became insensitive, distrustful and fearful. But why is it so hard for people to question that? Why do we follow the steps of others without inquiring what in the world we are doing? Why are we so afraid of being judged and put into the category of crazy or different? Why do we always want to fit in with the rest of the world?

I understand that in the past people were killed, burned or drowned when they practiced a different religion, a different belief, or disagreed with the science of the time, but that should not stop us from seeking our truth.

However, we carry an unconscious desire to belong to a group, or be part of something.

In order to do that, we believe we must compromise our own believes and accept everything that comes to us. The unconscious desire is nothing less than the yearning for a feeling of oneness, a connection with the rest, even if we do not know that this is what we are yearning for.

Of course, there were people who did stand up to face the world. People who many times had to sacrifice their entire lives. Those people who found the courage to show the world their ideas, their own thinking, even knowing that they would be removed from the *group* or called crazy and irrational. Those people, who many times were bullied or even killed, the ones who had the courage to stand up and say "this is wrong" or refuse to follow the standard. Thanks to them, we still have certain freedoms and have made great advances in science. Thanks to those who continue to follow their bliss and had faith in themselves, we now have more freedom to choose our own personal bliss. Unfortunately, there are many people who agree, we have been taught wrong, but are terrified to admit it in public or act upon it.

We need to learn to recognize what we are missing, and look inside of ourselves. We need to stop for one moment feel our own presence and use our own minds, recognize what are someone else's dogmas and what are our own beliefs and feelings on that matter. We must learn to listen to our heart, intuition and drive.

OUT OF TIME AND SPACE

Allow me to introduce the bigger part of myself that I am getting to know; a being that has always been present, but at the same time invisible to my own human eyes.

This being came to me through a revelation, like a memory of a big scenario that had always been there but that I never knew. I have come to the conclusion that even though this being is the bigger part of me, I know very little about it, because it goes beyond my human comprehension."

This revelation came to me at once but more details transpired as days passed. The message was overwhelming due to the intense emotions and large amount of information that made it difficult to translate in human words. But this is the best way to put it:

WE ARE COMPLETE!

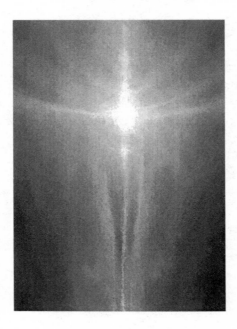

We have a plan, and we've been formulating this plan for a while. It is a dangerous plan, but we all understand the risks. We all know what can happen to us once we go there; we know nothing will ever be the same.

But we also know our intentions, we all know our reasons, so we must execute the plan now and not later. There are many universes among us, and they continue to expand. There is no beginning and no end to creation. It is endless and eternally expanding!

We are a small group of multidimensional light beings, who meet in our sacred place to implement our plan. We are free from pain because we have no physical bodies. We are light beings made of radiant white light, infused with celestial blue auras. What we are is vast but never-ending, for we continue to evolve just like everything else in the universes.

It is hard to describe our appearance or even what it feels

like to be what we are. *We are beyond human comprehension.*

We consciously choose to reincarnate and occupy physical bodies in order to execute our missions when needed. We understand the miracle of love.

Our intelligence is in tune with creation, we are pure creators who come from higher dimensions and travel from the none-physical universes to the physical with the purpose of expansion and love. We live outside time perimeters!

However, as we travel from the nonphysical to the physical, time still manifests as a bending and flexing energy wave of space and location.

There's a mutual feeling we all share as to why we're embarking on this mission. It is to raise the consciousness of unconditional love, the strongest force in the universes. The force that creates and connects everything! The force that moves our desire to share our knowledge and energy! *The meaning of creation, some might call it the source of life; others might call it God.*

As a conscious species we share this powerful feeling for all living beings. Our mission is to bring help to beings that go to earth or similar places and have fallen behind or gotten trapped. Some are young souls that wanted to expand their experiences; others are travelers from different universes working on projects.

However, there are also masters or beings of high consciousness who go to earth with a missionary purpose. For them the purpose is to serve and help by bringing change into the old wave of thought.

The masters of high consciousness continue their mission in periodic times, coming and going to earth until the mission is completed or the cycle is closed. Then they move to other realms of creation to begin their next mission.

The greatest risk for us after separation, would be to

become trapped in the physical body and forget the essence of what we are. We must awaken the enlightenment once again, but this time occupying a human body.

We must endure the experience of feeling trapped. Trapped in the illusion of time, trapped in the illusion of separateness. No matter how hard we would try to hold onto the knowledge of what we are, we must lose this memory once we incarnate in a flesh form, in order to regain it again.

The resurrection will grow the seed of enlightenment in that point of the universe, which is part of the great mission.

The love we feel for the souls and the earth is greater, much greater than the challenge ahead. We are complete beings, each one able to separate into multiple parts if needed. One part of us will be sent to the physical world (that part might divide itself into many incarnations with different genders, and different characteristics) and the biggest part will remain here, watching over the part that goes to earth. The part of us that stays out here will act as a guide together with the others. Our guidance will be crucial, but we will remain in the non-physical realm, and we will remain aware of self.

However, there will always be a connection between all parts, as they all belong to the same and together we make one.

The aware parts will remain connected to the incarnated souls and will provide guidance through messages and assistance in different ways whenever needed.

The incarnated soul must develop the understanding of its purpose on its own in order to give birth to the full realization of self. This is the goal ahead.

Every single incarnated-soul creates its own *map*, planning its journey ahead before engaging into the mission on earth. Every mission is unique and important without distinctions. *There is no small mission on earth.*

The incarnated-soul has a powerful mind that creates its reality because matter responds to the energy transmitted by the mind.

We'll stay together until the mission is complete. Even though we are individual entities, we unite our forces as one. We have faith in ourselves and we would never leave anyone behind, no matter how many reincarnations it may take an entity until it experiences the realization of self.

For the ones out here, time will feel like one intense wave of bounding moment. But for the ones on earth, it will feel as a never-ending eternity, because their bodies are affected by the physical law that creates the illusion of separation. Humans see time only in a linear way, when in reality, with some variations, all their reincarnations are happening simultaneously.

Once I become aware of self, while in the human body, I'll be able to alter the vibrational energy field between humans with the help of the group.

But the most important reason for me, is to be there for two precious beings who decided to engage into a journey to the land of alternative experience. Their goal is to transcend their souls' experience and help by stimulating the change that is needed on Earth. They have a big task ahead of them, an important mission, and I must help them succeed. Other light beings have volunteered before us, and have brought great change to earth, while some others got lost, distracted from their goal, and haven't come back. They're stuck in the heavy vibrational energy field. Those souls are lost, distracted, and have a hard time finding their way back.

Change is transitional and the planet's energy must change gradually and in its own time. The planet is crossing into the fourth dimension but it is mostly affected by the third, and with that, time and space play a big role.

We have been watching earth since its creation, and there

has been tremendous transformation in just a few millennium.

Earth is a living organism! It has a dense energy field. It's a planet going through a very important transition in its own evolution. It is time for earth to elevate its frequency in order to ascend to the next vibrational level. This will allow higher dimensions to coexist on earth and higher elements of thought within it. This transformation, again, must be gradual.

This planet is the perfect place for young souls to grow. It provides the opportunity for expansion in the celestial plain, for experiences to be achieved and realizations to be made. It is a place where the appearance of duality exist (the good and bad.) The soul uses these contrasts as a map to explore.

If I could only remember my true identity while I'm there, everything would be easier, but I know we're not supposed to remember. We must experience the absence of light, the absence of self.

We'll need to transcend the feeling of loss and the separation of self in order to be *reborn* to the realization of who we really are. The soul will experience separation from self, desperation, fear and death.

Even though the soul can never die, it will still need to experience such feelings.

The greatest realization of self will come gradually, one realization after another. It might take multiple simultaneous incarnations in different levels until the greatest realization takes place in the consciousness of the incarnated being.

Humans go through reincarnations with a sort of amnesia that has become difficult for them to overcome. There are multiple aspects to the human experience.

Pain and limitations will trigger the feeling that something is missing and needed in order to fulfill the life experience. The desire to find fulfillment and completion will be a motivator for the incarnated soul to continue searching for self. Once it finds the feeling of well-being, love and compassion, it will instinctively search for its source, and that eventually takes priority over all the apparent difficulties and endless cycles.

The soul knows that the bigger the challenge and experience, the bigger the realization, and therefore eagerly looks for that special scenario that will lead to this experience.

Incarnated souls will learn to experience all the feelings and sensations that only come from a place like earth and from having a physical body with its unique characteristics. The incarnated soul is always guided by its emotional system and its desires. It has everything it will ever need in order to experience a human life in awareness of self. It is always connected to its bigger part and has all the equipment and assistance it requires to communicate with the rest of the universes. It is never alone and would never be left behind.

The realization of the incarnated soul does not only accrue spiritual achievements, but also affects the human body and mind. Once the full realization is obtained by the incarnated soul, it will activate the brain neurons and receptors, awakening the brain's full capacity. That, in turn, will transform the chemistry of the body which will eventually evolve, affecting the DNA of the human species. This in turn, will allow the human body to receive and transmit higher frequencies. This energy will be transmitted fluently into the energy field and received by others on earth and in outer space.

The human body already carries the cell intelligence of a superhuman being. Its DNA requires the appropriate frequency stimulation in order for its receptors to awake to their full potential. One day humanity will understand its place in the cosmos. On that day, all eyes will be opened to other realities they are not aware of now. Dreams of super heroes with extraordinary abilities are based on a memory coming from the heart of a body that already carries the *potential to be.*

All beings that exist in the universes make one! Even when we all are unique individual creators, in the vast universes, we are also connected as one. One individual can never be apart from the rest. That does not mean we all occupy the same body. Individuality doesn't mean separateness, but it provides variety and uniqueness in unimaginable ways that create the potential to grow and expand. What affects one, affects the rest, what helps one, will also help the rest, like a *ripple effect.*
Life is in all, all is life!

INITIATION

This is the moment of engagement, the opportunity to serve the most divine of all purposes. I'm full of excitement, compassion, love and desire for this mission. Our group is in this moment engaging into a sacred ritual of high frequency that will allow the separation of a part of our souls.
This is a beautiful moment! The moment we have been waiting for, were a part of our soul will travel to Earth where the seed of an embryo is ready to receive the life of us to become an incarnated soul. In the name of love, so it is!

And then she was there, sitting down on the old mattress she had for a bed, resting her back against the brick wall......"

Intervention! (hear our message).

Don't try to make sense of what life appears to be through your human eyes, confusion will only follow; close your eyes and feel with your heart, trust that you have the greater capacity to perceive what your eyes can't!

SPIRIT GUIDES GUIDING:

I was around 15 years old, it was a warm summer day and I was tied up with house chores when something got my attention. I felt the need to go and look outside through the screen door that goes to the street. There was not much to see, other than a street full of houses, and old cars parked on both sides. Here and there, people walking on the street. Then I raise my sight to see beyond the houses, the mountains surrounding El Paso Texas. On top of one of them, people had build a star that shined during the night.

There was nothing specific on my mind, but suddenly I felt my first conscious premonition. It was a premonition that scared me at that time. I had an strong feeling that soon I would be living in the United States beyond those mountains.

I didn't like that feeling at that moment. I felt that soon I would need to leave my home and family, and that feeling scared me. It scared me because I did not want to leave my family, my school, my friends, my dreams, all the things I was working so hard to change.

I didn't know English and knew nothing about the US culture. So I wrote the premonition in my diary and tried to ignore it. I said to myself, "I will work very hard here where my mom and siblings are, so I don't ever have to leave." I was afraid that my mom would not have anybody to support her, and my youngest sisters and brothers would be in danger.

About three years later, I had just graduated from high school, and was working and taking extra courses to prepare for a test at a prestigious university. In my mind I had it all planed out. I thought, "I will study very hard, take the test, continue to work and go to the university, and one day I'll be able to have a career and help my family, one day I will be somebody."

I took the test and a few days later I went to the university to see my results.

When I saw my name on the list of people who passed the

test, I was so happy and proud of my big achievement, that I rushed home to tell my mom. This test was considered very difficult, so it was a big deal for me.

However, my happiness did not last long. The same week my mom informed me that my uncle from Kansas was in town. They were talking about our situation in Mexico, and he offered to take me with him so I could work in the United States and send money home.

My entire world collapsed when my mother told me about that conversation. She pointed out that this was a good opportunity for me to make more money than what I was making in Mexico, so I would be able to help her better. By then my parents were separated. When my father left the house he also stopped supporting us with money. My mom and I worked in a factory. Half of my earnings were going to school and the other half to the family. Since we were a family of eight children, that just was not enough.

My mother told me that I needed to make a decision soon because my uncle was going back to Kansas in a few days. It felt horrible but it was something I had to do. I loved my little brothers and sisters more than I loved my dreams. So, with my heart broken, *I chose to help my family and left my dreams behind*.

At that moment, I realized that my premonition from three years ago had just turned into reality.

Coming to the United States was easy, but not the transition into a new life. I was not ready for this change, but it turned out to be a blessing. Life in Mexico became even worse than what it already was. Poverty increased tremendously and so did crime.

A few years after I came to the United States the place where I was born turned into a battle field and a very dangerous area. There was a period of time when young women were killed and hundreds of bodies were found in different places. I couldn't believe it, it could have happened to me if I had chosen to stay.

This is what I mean when I say that sometimes interventions happen and I'm pushed to go in a different direction than what I had planned. I often have experienced, *interventions* in my life, situations that happened for a reason, and usually the reason is to keep me safe and alive, even against my own wishes and desires.

TODAY IS ALREADY YESTERDAY

I always wonder what time really means. Not necessarily the perception of one moment in time, but the linear time we got introduced to: Past, present and future.

Frequently I experience feelings of situations that have not yet happened but feel like they did. In other words, the feeling of what is about to happen. Many times I feel as if I am re-living a moment right when it is about to start. I usually go along with the feeling, knowing how it is going to transpire.

Sometimes I try changing something just to have fun; other times I feel as if someone is watching me from above. Strangely, it feels like it is I who observes.

Is there an explanation for this phenomenon? Does that mean that we can see into the future? Or does it mean that we already lived that moment?

Back in Mexico, in my early teens, I had an unusual dream. I was working in a factory building which housed several big assembly lines.

I saw a lot of unfamiliar people around me, there were more Caucasians and African-Americans than I ever seen before. But what got my attention in particular, was a bright yellow wall.

Even after waking up, the image of this wall stayed with me for awhile as if it wanted to burn itself into my memory. I wrote down the dream without putting too much attention to it because there was nothing familiar to me at that time.

Years later after I moved to the US, that same place I saw in my dream became my first official job. What a big surprise this was for me, to see the place exactly as I dreamed it.

In that moment that dream came back into my memory and it felt as if I had been there before and was just reliving the moment.

I recognized the same assembly lines, the people who worked there, and the big yellow wall. Does this mean that all the "déjà vu" I have experienced is something I dreamed of?

As many times as I have those sensations, I am not sure if they all happened in my dreams before I experienced them in my reality. But if they do happen during dreams, does that mean that our astral body is able to perceive the future, and if it does, how exactly is that happening?

I have seen future events through my dreams, but also during my awake hours. However, it can be a coincidence to have so many "déjà vu" sensations. The question is, what is really happening?

Many times I feel as if a bigger me is observing the little me here on earth from some point out there. In the moment that bigger me is observing, it feels like it can see through me from all angles or better said in a wide range or a fourth dimension.

When I become aware of it, I lose that brief connection that I had for a few seconds. I have experienced this "observer" many times during my awake hours. Sometimes I wonder if the phenomenon of being watched by myself from an above point, seeing future and past events through my dreams, and déjà vu experiences are actually phenomena that are constantly happening but I'm not aware of them. When I become aware of them, and I get a glimpse of the bigger picture, my mind attempts to make sense of those phenomena.

It is intriguing to imagine what else is happening in me and around me that I am not aware of, at least not just yet.

It is intriguing to me, that the universe is constantly transforming in front of my eyes and reacting to my own energy frequency without me seeing it with my physical eyes, until it becomes fully manifested.

We are amazing beings on the way to awareness!

Intervention! from the spirits of light

Do not be afraid of letting your desire come out of your heart. This is exactly what made you eager to come to earth. Allow your thought to manifest, do not hold yourself back. Close your eyes feel the vibration of your original intention that you sacredly hold in your heart.

OUR GUIDES INTERVENTIONS

Many of us have just began to explore the consequences of our own energy, our own thoughts, and our own frequencies. It is time to take responsibility for what we're creating and attracting into our own life.

Awareness is a gift and it's up to us to bring it into everything we do. If you think about it, it's not rocket science: Everything is energy and energy affects everything. That includes our electronics, our plants, our homes, and our bodies.

This is another amazing realization that we have now started "to play with" on a conscious level.

While I was working as an appraiser, one morning everything was going wrong for me. I had a hard time getting my equipment ready. I couldn't find the camera, the computer was acting weird and I couldn't open the map I needed, I was missing my special pencil and other items that I usually needed to do my job. As a result, I was running late.

My partner started to get mad at me because I was making her late too, since we used to go in pairs when going into questionable neighborhoods.

 When I finally got all of my things together, we went on the road. After appraising the first property, we went to the next house on our list but got stopped by the police who, had blocked the entrance to the street. We asked the officer what had happened and he informed us that there was a drive-by shooting about 15 or 20 minutes earlier. One person was shot and sent to the hospital.

If I had been on schedule that morning, my partner and I would have ended up in the middle of the shooting. In that moment, my misfortune of being late turned out to be a blessing. To me that was a clear intervention from my guardians who made me be late.

If it had been up to me, I would have left on time, and who knows what could have happened to us?

Intervention! From the spirits of light

Hear our thoughts; feel our presence, we are always with you and never apart. We are connected to you in forms that your human mind cannot comprehend. We are please that you have started to understand the being that you are, and soon you will understand what we are together.

LET'S TALK ABOUT THE HUMAN MIND FOR A MOMENT

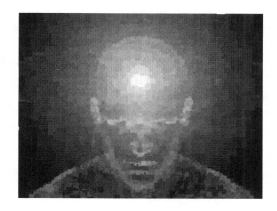

I was always intrigued by what we call "reality" and how our mind reacts to it. Think about it! in order to be in the physical world, we must have the appropriate tools to participate in the experience.

We have a powerful brain, a tool that continues to evolve with time, a super sophisticated machine that is capable of learning anything we want. It has so many complex functions and operations; it communicates and gives orders to the body and will do anything to keep itself alive.

The brain produces, organizes and distributes countless, pieces of information per second. It has receptors that act like antennas, always receiving and transmitting data. The brain is such a sophisticated machine, it does all of its functions independently, with no need or reminders from us, it just does it on its own.

The amazing brain is intimately connected with the life source occupying the body, *the incarnated soul.*

The human body, the temple of the soul, is an intelligent organism, composed of trillions of cells working together in perfect harmony. Every cell carries the DNA of life.

The human body has multiple energy points also known as chakras, where energy is received and transmitted. There is independent cell intelligence that goes beyond our comprehension. On the evolutionary scale we are still children who continue to grow the understanding of what we are.

Our bodies are already equipped with the tools we need, we just don't know how to use them yet.

Unfortunately, this is one of the reasons why we hurt ourselves and others in the process of learning. We are like children playing with a powerful gun, not understanding the dangers and the potential our minds possess.

Many people believe the mind is the enemy because it never stops the process of thinking. The mind gets distracted and is always wondering, flying from place to

place, from memory to memory, from past to future,
wondering from project to project.

Many believe the mind acts on its own and can overpower
our will, take us to a painful past memory, and keep us
there to suffer. There is so much we don't know about
ourselves, and the mind is a big part of it.

As we have learned in school, when an individual is
cognitively tested and the answers are rational, it means
that this individual is *ok* and fits into the *normal standards*
society has established. If that individual would answer
with what are called irrational responses, our doctors would
categorize the person as disturbed or psychotic, and
prescribe medicine to suppress such distortions and
delusions of the mind.

But when is the mind sick and when is the mind actually
dipping into other realities? We are far from understanding
the subconscious and conscious parts of the mind. For
example, we as a society have trained the mind to *believe*
that we are not capable of seeing or feeling other energy
beings among us. We have been trained to ignore our own
sensory perception, to ignore our bodies frequencies and
the frequencies of the planet.

We have limited our precious minds to believe only in what
is called *rational*, the subconscious is the mystery part of
the mind that is intimately connected with the self and the
universes.

When the mind tries to suppress a feeling, or its own truth,
our subconscious reacts in inconceivable ways, trying to
come to the surface, creating distortions or side effects.

My personal believe is that we got it all wrong! The mind is
not the enemy! On the contrary, the mind is an amazing
tool. And if the mind is not working at the capacity we
would like it to, it is because we are the trainers and we
have failed to train it properly.

Instead, we have fed it *junk food*. I believe that everything we are born with on this planet is there for a reason, and the reason is to serve us in our experience on earth.

The body cannot live without the mind, the mind cannot live without the spirit, and the spirit is an extension of the soul. If we think about it, our minds have given us many signs of discomfort during our lifetimes, but we haven't paid enough attention.

When we feed our minds with garbage like wrong beliefs, limitations and fears, our minds develop side effects and illnesses.

We need to change our minds diet and start feeding them with healthier thoughts, but that is easier said than done.

Remember, the reality that we are living is the perception of what the mind believes, and, again the mind has its believes because that's what we have accepted as truth. Imagine changing that perception to a limitless reality, a reality were we have freed our minds from all kinds of restrictions and limitations, a reality where everything is possible, a reality where we love and accept ourselves, where we engage in an amazing journey of self-discovery, where we feel powerful, and complete.

We must learn to accept that we are *powerful, amazing, energy beings*. If the mind is capable of understanding that there are other possibilities in what we call reality, then it is possible for the mind to transcend limitations. The mind will do amazing things when acceptance has grown strong roots in the brain.

If you think about it, everything in the universes is alive and constantly changing, as if it had a mind of its own or is ruled by a supreme universal law. We were not born with an enemy attached to us. We were not born with the purpose of being here to suffer, to be tormented or destroyed by unseen forces. We are here to experience, explore, expand, discover and enjoy life.

Our bodies, brains and minds are made out of the earth elements and the spirit of the universes! In short, we have suppressed, missed trained, mislead, misused, and more than anything misunderstood the mind. We have trained the mind to believe false information. Consequently, the mind has responded to what it has learned and continues to play the distortions that we ended up believing.

All the garbage that was put in our minds since childhood, and that we continued to add later, is holding us down. As a result, the mind continues to replay the wrong information in our heads over and over in order to continue fulfilling its purpose, the purpose of serving us, that consequently made us believe the lies we taught to our minds, transforming us into fearful creatures.

In the end we have become afraid of the mind and talk about it as if it is something that doesn't belong to us, like a tumor that we want to get rid of. In reality, the mind has always been there to serve us.

The mind is not there to stop us on our path to enlightenment, or to make it tricky for us to get there. The mind is only providing us with information and beliefs that we have fed it with, no more, no less.

If you think about it, the amazing mind gives meaning to everything and is always learning. If focused on a goal, the mind is able to make miracles happen, overcome illness, overcome problems or disabilities.

The amazing mind gives us the opportunity to make choices in life, to choose what is right or wrong, or help us to make logical decisions. It connects with anything or anyone we choose to connect with just by thinking about it or by using our imagination, no matter the distance.

Thanks to the mind, somebody had the imagination to create the first plane, the first radio, and television. All kinds of inventions come from someone's mind. The mind, that if it is trained to believe that anything is possible, will allow us to fly through the sky without wings, walk on water, and awaken our superhuman abilities, ignoring the laws of physics.

The mind, if set to a specific belief or vibration, is capable of self-healing terminal illnesses. The amazing mind that, if trained well, is capable of taking us to higher dimensions if we allow it to function to its full capacity. The amazing mind allows the imagination to fly and give life to thoughts, thoughts that create worlds!

On the opposite side, years later I realized just how dangerous our mind can be to us when we feed it with wrong information.

One day, I was cleaning the house, vacuuming, when I heard somebody knocking. I opened the door and was surprised to see Gabriel, a friend of mine. "Do you have a moment?, Can we go inside and talk?". Stepping aside, I was pointing to the living room, "Sure, come in." As Gabriel was passing by me on his way into the house, as strong current of energy almost knocked me over rushing in with him.

After sitting down, Gabriel looked me into the eyes and started: "I have bad news. Hegel was rushed to the hospital yesterday evening and passed away during the night." Hegel, a mutual friend of mine and Gabriel suffered from a heart decease for years but had so far avoided to get into serious trouble.

After sharing more details about the circumstances of Hegel's passing and some specifics about the funeral arrangements, Gabriel went his way, and left me with the energy I by now had realized was Hegel.

Days later, I was still feeling his energy. By now it started to annoy me because it prevented me from sleeping and made my house feel restless.

As an attempt to resolve this problem, I started to meditate to get into contact with Hegel to give him a message. I was simply trying to help him, by guiding him into the light. However, it didn't seem to work.

One night, my sleep was interrupted by the feeling of somebody shaking me, trying to wake me up. Sitting up, I again detected Hegel's energy in the room.

Taking a deep breath, I said, "I give up, what do you want?"

Feeling only the same restless energy that I felt the last few days, I continued.

"OK, why don't you take me with you in a dream and we can try to figure this out together."

That said, I turned around, closed my eyes and went back to sleep within minutes.

Opening my eyes, I found myself in a strange area I didn't recognize. It was dark, but I could make out the mountains in the distance and the rolling landscape along my sides. In front of me, Hegel seemed very excited to see me and welcomed me with a warm hug. "Thank you for coming, I missed you."

"What is the problem, what is going on, why can't you see the light?" I asked confused.

"There is no damn light!" Sounding desperate, he mentioned, "there is only this, nothing else"

Then he said. "Hurry up, we need to hide before they come!"

At that moment, the air around us felt like it became infused with negative energy, and all the people that shared this space with us tried to get away, looking for cover.

Ignoring the towering something behind me, Hegel grabbed my hand and started to pull me behind a bolder next to the path. I was terrified with what was happening, but after a moment of gathering my thoughts, I told Hegel, "we need to fight back, we can't just hide."

Hegel was shocked, "Are you crazy?"

Not knowing where this came from, I told him "What do you have to lose? You are already dead!" That seemed to throw him of guard, because he was standing there for a few moments, just looking at me with a blank stare.

Not waiting for him, I left the safety of the bolder, and walked back onto the path to face whatever was coming our way. That was the moment I woke up and realized, that Hegel had taken me up on my offer to show me, why he hadn't moved on.

Sorting through the dream, I realized that his issues came from the facts that his death not only caught him by surprise, he also was afraid of what's next.

His mind was in a terrible place, keeping him locked in a loop of fear, and the resulting images this fear created. Together with other like minded people, not able to comprehend what was happening around them, they kept reflecting on the distortion of their minds, creating the most horrible scenarios that haunted them.

Later on I realized that here on earth and in the next place after "death" we continue to keep our emotions and desires with us, specially our fears and believes. That is exactly the problem, once we die, we continue to keep the same way of thinking of what we once believed while on earth "until we're able to "move on." By not having a material world made of atoms, manifesting our fears becomes the easiest thing to do.

I understood later why my friend was upset at me when I kept telling him to "go to the light" when to him there was no light to go too, and there were more people like him attracting each other and manifesting at great capacity everything they were afraid of.

Another thing I realized was that dead people are able to see the living easier that it is for us the other way around. My friend kept visiting so many times because by me calling to my guides and guardians he felt a sense of comfort. Hegel's' transition was difficult in the beginning but later one he started to free himself from the initial fear and started to let go more and more until finally he crossed over.

Ironically we should not follow the light, instead, we should actually call for it. Not only after we died but especially while we are here on earth, because here is where we came to embrace the beings of light that we truly are.

The light is not a physical Phenomenon that will appear in front of us, instead it will come from inside.

Remember, in this plane and in the next one, it is your powerful mind projecting thoughts that materialize into matter out of plain air. Many times, our thoughts are what keep us in the shadows, because "we are were our attention goes." This is the time to retrain our powerful-mind, here in the right now, and bring thoughts of light and thoughts of love.

What we are feeding our minds is extremely important, because the way we see life, how we feel about it, and what we think of it, becomes our conscious level.

When we start to practice positive thoughts on a daily base or every time that we remember, we make it a habit, and our life will start to change and we will attract the good in many different ways.

There's much more the mind can do but we must stop seeing it as if it is something negative. By doing so, it reflects exactly what we are creating. Remember, the power of the mind is unlimited, unless we give it a limit. The mind is an amazing tool and it is up to us how we use it and what we do with it. We are intelligent creatures, amazing energy beings that, as we continue to discover ourselves and our capabilities, we can open doors to new worlds of understanding of what we are!

Intervention! From the spirits of light

Desire + imagination+ believe + will = the creation of something. The incarnated soul uses the mind as a tool to direct energy to a point of creation. Everything is sacredly entangled including multiple dimensions and parallel universes. The mind is also a tool for the incarnated soul to move between dimensions, explore new worlds within it, and create and give form to life.

I FELT ASHAMED, BUT WHY?

I want to share with you a memory that I used to be ashamed of. I was around 17 years old, still living in Mexico. My father had recently left the house to live his own life, leaving my mother with all the children and no financial support. the youngest of my siblings, was barely one year old.

One day, my mother took one of my sisters with her to get groceries and left me in charge of the rest of my siblings. "Lock the door," she said " and if your father comes, don't let him in, I'm afraid he will take the baby."

As expected, my father, knocked at the door, telling my mother to let him in. I told my father that she wasn't there and to come back after she returned. My father cursed at me "I'm here with a policeman. I want my things," he said. "Let him in" the other man grumbled. The kids were scared, my father and the other guy yelled and hit the door repeatedly.

I moved the kids into one area of the room so my father wouldn't try to hurt them or take them, and opened the door. They were both drunk.

My father rushed into the room, calling me names, while the other man said "just let him get his things out." I saw a gun under his vest.

After getting his things, my father tried to take the baby with him, but I stopped him telling him that he could not take the baby. He slapped me very hard in the face.

In that moment I felt an intense hate all through my body that gave me strength to confront my father. I raised my hand and slapped him back. "Leave the house now," I yelled. My father looked at me, took his clothes and walked away.

When the danger had passed and my anger calmed down, I felt ashamed of what I did to my father.

Even knowing that I was right to defend my siblings, I couldn't help but feel ashamed for raising my hand against him.

I used to think that memories like this one about my childhood and teenage years while I was living with my parents, were too dramatic and sad to be told. I kept them to myself for a long time, hoping nobody saw through me.
I was ashamed and depressed about those memories. After all, people want to hear happy and successful stories, so I showed the world a different face, the face of a strong person who refused to make herself a victim of her own past or future. However, it took me many years to understand that it is OK to feel vulnerable, ashamed or hurt and to take those lessons as an experience.
I learned to accept my past, dust myself off and heal my own wounds.

Intervention! From the spirits of light

*Creator of life I am in you! Leave the path of doubt and
follow me. Trust a little more and you will be able to see
what you couldn't before, creator of life I am in you.
You are my experience, the source that gives life to my
expansion in the universe. I am the intelligence the source
of life that created you. Without me you cannot exist,
without you I could never expand. Creator of life I am in
you.*

NO ONE TO BLAME

I've reached a point in my life where I'm finally understanding a little more about me. Should I call it awareness or should I not give it a name? It doesn't matter; what really matters is the liberating feeling this realization brings.

I realize that I never really loved myself, *unconditionally*. I never really appreciated the being that I am. I never treated myself as I should have. Instead, I did the opposite. I expected others to appreciate me. I expected others to treat me well and love me unconditionally and felt hurt when they didn't.

There's no one to blame, because I am the creator of my own reality. Everything that surrounds me in this moment is what I have attracted and manifested.

If I want something to change, it is up to me to direct my desire to that path and allow myself to receive.

I am beginning to understand how everything is connected. Nothing is separate from the rest.

All the contrast is part of what we create. There is no good or bad until we give it a judgment.

This realization is absolutely amazing! It's amazing to know that we have all the power in our hands to make changes in our lives.

There is no reason to be afraid!

I have seen the past, the present and the future in my dreams. We are more than what we think we are. We are strangers in our own bodies. Strangers to our own selves, it feels like we're suffering from some kind of amnesia. We think we know who we are by how we define ourselves in society, by getting a degree and calling ourselves doctors, mechanics or whatever our profession becomes.

We give ourselves titles and brand ourselves to show that we belong to some specialization or group. We trust our doctors, our politicians, our priests even our horoscopes, more than we trust ourselves.

We join multiple groups trying to fit with the rest so we won't be viewed as different by others.

 I realized that most of what moves us is fear: Fear of being alone, fear of being left behind, fear of making mistakes and being questioned or punished by the ones who claim to know more about something when in reality we are afraid of our own selves, afraid of what we may find in the darkness of our shadows.
We are afraid of the invisible, because we haven't realized who we really are.

One morning I woke up in a lot of pain. My body was aching all over and I felt pity for myself. "why does life keep putting me down?" I asked myself. "I work hard, I do good things for others, and in fact the story of my life since childhood is to put others before me. I have sacrificed many things in life so others can have it better.

Why am I having this karma? Why am I being punished? What am I doing wrong?"
Then I stopped, and asked myself; "What am I saying?" I realized there is no punisher in my dictionary. I realized I was judging my situation as good or bad, and also by merit. Analyzing my thoughts, I realized I made myself a victim of circumstances. I realized there was no one to blame and nothing to judge, it was only an experience, and the experience, regardless of whether I liked it or not, was what I attracted to my life.
With that realization I embraced the present moment with everything that came with it, and blessed it.

Intervention! From the spirits of light

Do not pray, do not beg, do not condemn yourself, and do not offer a sacrifice. Just silence your mind, close your eyes, feel our presence. We are never apart and always with you! Remember who you are and take back your power!

ENCOUNTER WITH ONE OF MY GUIDES

At another time I was sleeping in my room, dreaming that I was sitting in bed listening to one of my guides.

In my eyes he was the picture of a wise, old man, with long white hair and a full beard.

While he was talking to me, I felt overwhelmed with love, respect and admiration for him. Apparently he was teaching me, guiding me on something.

In my dream I felt that I had known him for a long time, and that feeling made me very comfortable. I felt as if this were another encounter out of many others we already had. His presence created such a peaceful environment, radiating wisdom, love and tranquility.

In the dream I began to ask him something, when he raised his finger to his lips, gesturing to me to be silent. "Listen," he said, I asked "to what?" "There is a spirit passing by in this very moment, listen."

And I did, I heard steps coming from the living room to the hallway and stopping in front of my room. I woke up with the sensation that someone had entered my room and was looking at me.

I didn't see anyone , but was able to remember the part of my dream with the wise man.

It was a great feeling to know that I had such a vivid encounter with a guide, but it also felt sad that my encounters were not memories that I could bring into my consciousness when I needed them. If it wouldn't have been for the *ghost* waking me up, I wouldn't have been able to remember my encounter with my spirit guide visiting me in the astral plane.

My guide communicated with me on a subconscious level, which is not fair to my little mind that has problems understanding these things! My little mind struggles to understand the *big picture* of who I am. My little mind has very little faith and suffers because of that. It has gone through so many miracles that happened to me in this life, but still it easily forgets. It has come to many realizations but still has a lot of room for more. One of my purposes in life is to love and accept myself with everything that makes me what I am.

THE VOICE FROM THE HEART

The heart is one of the most important organs in the human body. The heart is the first organ to be created from the time of conception and one of the most powerful tools we posses. It retains half of the original cell that an embryo comes from, along with that brain, it is another organ that we do not know how to use.

Through the heart we hear the voice of love, and through love we can connect to the self and the universes. Most of the time the heart doesn't understand the mind and vice-versa.
The heart lives in the present moment and expresses feelings through emotions and desires. It has no judgment, no agenda. Through the heart and its feelings of love, we can experience the desire to help others.

When a person allows herself to love herself, this person becomes capable of loving others.
Love is the most powerful force in the universes; this energy frequency called *love* can heal illnesses or guide the well being of others without a second thought or *what is in it for me*.
I mentioned earlier that the mind can heal its own body by having the willpower to do it, but a person cannot heal another human being through will power; instead he must use the *ultimate weapon* which is love.
If the person who is ill allows him/herself to receive healing from the universes, that person will heal because every cell reacts to the frequency of love. Our cells are intelligent and receptive. When the intention of love and wellbeing is expressed towards a sick person, it will help the affected cells to receive the love that is offered and to regenerate themselves.
We all carry the power of healing within our cells, and a way to transmit it to others is through the feeling of love, the pure intention of love directed toward another human

being.
When we learn to connect the mind, the heart and the spirit, powerful manifestations happen.

According to my guides, it is all part of the package!

Intervention! From the spirits of light

"Creator of life I am in you! Leave the path of doubt and follow me. Trust a little more and you will be able to see what you couldn't before. Creator of life I am in you. You are my experience, the source that gives life to my expansion in the universe. I'm the intelligence, the source of life that created you. Without me you cannot exist, without you I could never expand. Creator of life I am in you."

OUR OWN GUIDANCE

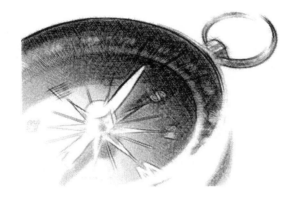

I believe we are all born with some sort of guidance, even though many times it is hard to listen to what the heart is feeling.

When I was younger, many times I doubted myself and my ability to connect with my feelings; later in life, the connection to myself was clear and direct.

There were also times when I was forced to do something I didn't want to do, but circumstances required immediate action. Most of the time it became clear a few days or months later, when events showed me what could have been the consequences if I hadn't have taken those actions. It felt as if someone had guided me to do it.

Let me share another childhood experience with you, an experience that I called *The black spider web*.

One night I was laying in the one bed we all shared, submersed in a deep sleep, when the feeling of myself re-entering the body woke me up abruptly. Sitting up in bed, I opened my eyes but couldn't see anything.

The room was dark and filled with smoke. Coughing, I called my mother and siblings, trying to wake them up. My mother responded first, "oh my God, the heater burned out and is overheating." Immediately she got up, opened the door and the window, and carried the heater outside. "Are you kids ok?" she asked. By then my siblings were awake and coughing . When my mother turned on the light we all had inhaled so much smoke, that we had the residue tracks under our noses.

Being a typical eight year old, I didn't pay attention to the fact that we all could have died in this room; no, what got my attention, were the black spider webs hanging from the ceiling.

Looking back from the perspective of an adult, it amazes me more to realize what woke me up! Being asleep, and away in astral form, I was rushed back into my physical body by my bigger self, to wake up and prevent harm from the danger that was facing us.

We must learn to believe that we are always guided, and give ourselves a chance to experience the feeling of being taken care of, no matter how events might appear: The loss of loved ones, illness or disabilities, or other apparent misfortunes.

Our hearts are yearning for the love that can only be fulfilled by the love to ourselves, but how can we love someone that we do not know?

I realized that talking to ourselves is easy, anyone can start a dialogue with oneself with no problem, but listening and understanding the feelings that come from the heart is a different story. I and many others grew up believing that if we want to talk to *God* we should go to church, and if we need to ask him for something, we should get on our knees and cry, beg, and promise that we will give up something or offer some sort of sacrifice. We grew up getting more and more away from ourselves.

Fortunately, we do not need to go anywhere; no need to find a *guru* or go to Tibet. What we need to do, is to silence our mind and learn to listen to the heart.

In the beginning of this book, I mentioned that when I was a teenager I hoped someone would show me the way. Indeed, I was hoping to find my own *guru*, someone to make things clear for me and tell me what to do. How ironic! As I have grown older in wisdom and learned from my own experiences, I run away every time someone tries to *show me the way*. This is precisely what I subconsciously avoided all of my life, someone else thinking for me, someone else taking away my right to freely come to my own conclusion about what I should believe.

Of course we can always learn from each other, keeping an

open mind and listening to ideas and beliefs, but it is up to us to digest those ideas, grab what feels good for us in that moment, and let go of the rest.

Don't follow the guru; instead, become your own!

Intervention! From the spirits of light

*The reality that you know, is the reality you have created
for yourselves. We all participate as a collective soul. The
individual souls have a common agreement to the
expansion of life. Allow yourself to feel the intensity of this
moment with all that it has; the intensity of this experience
with all that it is, for this contains the answers you were
looking for.*

THE MYSTERY OR REINCARNATION

Many mysteries within ourselves are difficult to understand because we were not trained to do so by society. One of those mysteries is reincarnation.

Many people ridicule the idea of living more than one life. I believe reincarnation is a fact, and many times experiences from a past life are connected to the present.

Reincarnation memories might come to us in different ways. Many times, one can feel affinity and love for other people, as well as hate or discomfort towards them. Many times, we are born knowing how to play an instrument or possess some kind of skills, while other times we are born with bodily pain and disabilities without injuries being present or any other apparent reason.
By studying mine and other people's scenarios, I came to the realization that reincarnation is real. My experiences have come to me sometimes through dreams, but also in my waking hours, triggering intense emotions that can only be explained as a past or future life experience.

Why do we reincarnate multiple times, and what do we get out of it? Those have been questions that motivated me to explore more about the subject. I believe no one can reach the total understanding of reincarnation until we are out of *the cycle*. However, I can clearly see that the simple fact of living under different genders or certain characteristics creates a unique experience that allows us to understand what life on earth can be.

Let me share some of those experiences with you.
In those experiences I was dressed in old clothes accurately reflecting a different era and each scenario indicated different places and circumstances. Two of these experiences came to me in form of a dream.

Reincarnation As a *Young Girl.*

I was a thin young woman, maybe sixteen or seventeen, with long brown and curly hair, white skin, and clear eyes. My parents chose my husband and married me to that man in exchange for land. This man was in his early forties, dark hair, tall and solid. He was also wealthy and popular. To him, I became his property, the perfect wife he wanted to have children with.

There was no love in this union. I remember being very scared of him. He took me to a big house out in the country that had many rooms. My bedroom had a backdoor to a garden where I spent most of my time in order to avoid him.

In my dream, I saw myself as that girl, sitting somewhere in the garden crying because I didn't want to be there, or to be married to that man. I could not count on my parents support; on the contrary, they warned me to be a good wife. Even though he spent most of the day out of the house, I knew that eventually he would come back home at night. When he did, he usually was drunk and many times he forced me to be intimate with him. He abused me physically, leaving bruises on my face and body. I remember being too embarrassed to go downstairs to eat because I didn't want the servants to see me like that.

But one of the servants, even though she was also afraid of my husband, felt pity for me. She was in her mid forties, dark hair and heavy figure. Many times she helped me taking care of the bruises and bringing me food.

One day, seeing me crying, she offered to help me escape. While planning, she told me she would not leave me by myself and offered to come with me. I was very grateful to that woman who, knowing that she could get hurt, still tried to help me.

The plan was to take the train and go far away, but we didn't make it. Right before we got to the train station my husband found out where we were, and furiously confronted and killed us both.

That was not just a dream! I knew that girl was me in a different time. During the dream, I was living the experience but also observing from somewhere else outside of my body (as if I was watching my own movie). I was that person and the observer at the same time.

I remember the dream vividly but I don't remember dying or how I died. I only remember, that he killed us both. When I woke up, I felt such a relief that it was over, and that I was still alive. And I remembered the fear and emotions this young girl felt until the end of her life.

I believe I dipped into my first past life experience, and as time passed by, I continued to have similar revelations like this.

Reincarnation As *a Man*.

I was a middle aged man in my forties, with dark hair, a thick body, and full of plans for the future. In my dream, it was a cold afternoon and I was wearing a heavy coat with big buttons. I saw myself in an empty building where the fifth or sixth floor was still under construction. Like most floors, it was missing the walls.

I went there to meet my business partner and a friend of his I never met before who was dressed as a priest. We were talking about business and began to argue. Too late, I realized that I was *set up*. My partner had other intentions for me when I confronted him about being dishonest. He and the supposed priest were there to kill me.

We started yelling at each other and the argument turned to a fight. When we paused for a moment, I turned my back to them, trying to collect my thoughts ,when one of them pushed me out of the building.

Next thing I remember, I heard the ambulance, and moments later the doctors and nurses rushed me through the hospital hallway. They got me into a room filled with medical equipment, and while they were doing their best to keep me alive, I saw my spirit separating from my body, as if my body wasn't able to hold it anymore. A moment later, they declared me dead.

I remember a feeling of deep sadness because I saw my future breaking apart in front of me while there still where so many plans ahead. All I wanted at this moment was to see my family again. Then I lost my sense of time. The next thing I remember is seeing my spirit visiting the family.
I entered a house and saw my son and daughter, both in their twenties, sitting in chairs, dressed in black and very upset, mourning the death of their father. Then my spirit entered into a bedroom and I saw my wife lying in bed. She also was wearing black, crying about the loss of her husband. I gently laid down by her side holding her with so much love and sadness, hoping she would feel my presence, wanting her to know that I was there and that I loved her very much and that I was sad for leaving her like that.
Waking up, I felt sad about what had just happened in my dream. Again, it felt as if I were living the experience while watching *me* at the same time as the events unfolded.
In the dream I was the observer of something that had to happen and I was not allowed to change anything about the experience, only to observe.
As the person having the experience, I felt all sorts of emotions as I went through those circumstances. I felt betrayed by a business partner, saw how my life ended drastically, and felt heartbroken about leaving my family alone. In the dream, I was not ready to die!
I asked myself what all of this means. Frequently, I experience observing myself, through an astral body, while going through the day. However, as soon as I become aware of the *observer* I lose the connection to that part of me that was observing.

Past Life Experience with a *Dear Friend*.

I have a friend who's been in my life for many years. When I first met her I was attracted to her energy because she was always happy and cheerful. We have been in each other's lives for many years. We have gone through life together, experiencing different relationships, happiness, sadness, children, and vacations.

We are both very curious about life, and that curiosity awoke a desire to learn different philosophies, one of them was Wicca. We wanted to see for ourselves what Wicca really was. Half of my friend's ancestors were Native Americans and therefore she firmly believes in honoring the earth.

We learned many good lessons and were surprised how much good could come from teachings such as honoring mother earth, and respecting life and the elements. My friend and I always felt very close to each other, as if we knew each other from somewhere else.

One night we did a ritual to see if we could find our past life roots. We wanted to know if we met before at a different time. We performed the ritual and we both went into some sort of trance, leading to simultaneous experiences.

My experience was that my friend and I were young, maybe in our late teens (it felt like watching a movie inside my head). I saw both of us somewhere in Europe, dressing very differently. We had long dresses, long hair and were surrounded by lots of pine trees.

We were friends, beautiful young girls, and full of life. I recognized her by her happy spirit. We lived in a little village and we were much attuned with the planet. Along with our mothers and relatives, we worked with herbs and nature; some people called us medicine women, while others mistakenly called us witches.

Then my vision went from happy to sad, I saw both of us running away, trying to escape from a group of people who wanted to hurt us. At the end, we were captured and they brutally took our lives. When we came out of trance, my friend and I shared the same story and we were describing the same landscape, the same vision of how we looked in the past and how we dressed, what we were doing, and how we were killed.

I will never forget that experience, not only because we both saw the same thing but also for how we died. That explained to me why I care so much about my friend.

Present Life Experiences - The Love of my Life

In this life experience I had the opportunity to meet many people I meet in other reincarnations. My husband is one of those, we share a special love and connection to each other. Let me tell you a little story about my husband and I. Planning our wedding, we both were drawn to a medieval theme. So we tried using medieval items wherever possible. Cups, knives, candles, invitations, wardrobe, and we even found a little chapel that looked like it was built in medieval times.

For our honeymoon we went to Germany, visiting my husband's birth place with no specific destination afterwards. However, I had an intense desire to see German castles. We visited several majestic palaces and castles, but I kept having the feeling I was not finding what I was looking for.

All the places we visited were beautiful, but missing something, and I didn't know what.

Apparently my husband was feeling the same way. He started to search the internet for more castles to visit. He found a castle that was in ruins but for the most part still standing. This castle was built in the 11th century and rebuilt later on.

When we entered through the first big door, a ton of feelings came to me, emotions and excitement, that I had not felt before in any of the other castles.

I had the feeling that I was back home. It felt as if I were in a place where I hadn't been for a long time and always wanted to come back to.

I felt that this was my home in a past time, everything was so familiar. I started having memories of people and children who lived within the castle, and to my surprise my husband was also my husband in that past life. He was a knight and I was his wife.

My heart was beating fast as I was having those memories, but I did not say anything to my husband, who also seemed to be having his own experience.

In my memories I remember my husband and me living in the castle, loving each other very much.

As part of being a knight, my husband had to leave frequently to go into battle. For years, he returned after every fight, but one day he was sent out and never came back. He got killed and never had the chance to see our son grow up.

 I don't remember most of what happened after that, but I remember feeling very sad the day I had to leave the castle with our son. I had so many memories of that time with my husband and the *glory days* in the castle.

Going back together to our *old home* brought back all kinds of emotions.

Without yet sharing my experience with my husband, I asked him what he thought of the place, and to my surprise he told me that he felt like we had been here together in a different time.

My husband is not the kind of person who gets premonitions or feelings like this, but even he had memories of us in one specific area of the castle.

I told him what I experienced, my emotions, feelings and images that came to me as if they were memories of a life I used to have with him. We were both amazed at what we had uncovered.

Suddenly everything clicked; we started to understand how everything in our present life was connected to the past. Our medieval wedding style, the desire to visit Germany to look for castles, and how we ended up finding this one, as if something was guiding us to this specific location. But the greatest discovery was that we found each other again in this life and were drawn back to the castle, our past home.

I couldn't help but feel grateful and fortunate for meeting my husband one more time and to having the opportunity to live together and share another life experience.

SEEING THE FUTURE

Many years ago, when my children were still toddlers and I was living with their father, I had a very strange dream. In this dream, I was a single mom buying a house.

I saw my children, who were about 11 or 12 years old, looking so different and grown up.

In my dream, we went to look at a house with a female realtor. For some reason she was not able to open the front door, so she said "let's go to the side and enter through the basement door." Entering the house through the basement and making our way up to the second floor, we fell in love with the house and ended up buying it.

In the same dream, while living in the house, one night I heard noises in the basement and went there while my children and my mother, who was staying with us for some time, where asleep in the upstairs rooms.

Stepping into the basement, I saw a woman hiding in the shadows and I realized she was a ghost.

To my surprise, she seemed to recognize me. She grabbed me by the arm and told me that we needed to leave. She didn't seem to be bothered by the blood that covered more than half of her head. I guess she had not recognized the fact that she was dead, because she still tried to get us out of the room in a hurry.

Her eyes were filled with fear. I told her she was confusing me with somebody else, but she firmly said "No, that is not possible, we need to hurry up before he finds us and kills us both." I said "Lady, I'm not who you think I am," but she insisted, "Yes you are," and pulled some pictures out of her sweater's pocket, pointing at them. "See, this is you."

I looked at the pictures and to my surprise, the girl in there was the same girl I dreamed about earlier that tried to escape from her husband and was killed along with the woman helping her. Suddenly all the memories from that life came back.

I understood why this woman was scared to death and why

she recognized me. She was the woman helping me escape. I felt so much loyalty to her, because she risked her own life just to help me escape. I looked her in the eyes, holding her arm, and kindly explained to her that I now remembered everything that happened, but also that everything had changed, I was now a different person in a different time and she was dead and needed to realize that so she could move on.

I told her not to be scared anymore, because he no longer could hurt us.

The moment she started realizing that everything had changed, the look of fear and confusion left her face and she started to vanish into thin air the moment she let go of my arm.

When I woke up from that dream I was very confused. First of all why was I a single parent, and why did my children look so different and grown up? Not to mention, why the ghost from the basement was the same woman who helped me escape in a past life. As usual, I ended up writing down my dream into my diary.

The weird part is that this dream came true. When my children were 11 and 12 years old, I was a single mom looking for a house. After looking at different houses I found one that got my attention. It looked perfect for my children to grow up in, so I asked my realtor to show me the house. When we went there she tried opening the front door but the key didn't work, so she said "Let's go through the basement door." When she opened the door, I started to feel all kinds of emotions. Memories of the dream I had so many years ago started to come back to me, and I knew this was meant to be my house.

The circumstances, like the front door not opening, and my children looking just like they did, were exactly as the dream I had many years ago. Without hesitation, I told my realtor to put an offer on the house, knowing it was meant to be mine. Needless to say, my children and I spent many happy years in this house.

THE OBSERVER: present time

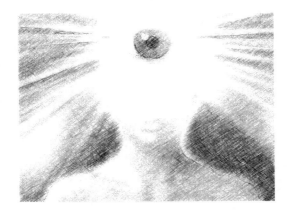

Going back to the observer, I had a unique encounter in which I experienced myself being in three places at the same time.

It is hard to describe but this is how it started:

One morning I was lying in bed facing the ceiling. I opened my eyes, feeling that someone was looking at me. It felt as if I was just coming out of the dream stage. I saw a familiar being observing me from above. This being had so much love for me, it was almost overwhelming.

This being felt extremely powerful. I became amazed just looking at it for a few seconds, mesmerized by the feelings it was transmitting to me. With its mind, it told me that I needed to wake up because I was having a dream that was getting ready to turn into a nightmare. Then it pointed past me.

Following its gesture, I saw myself dreaming and realized how the dream started to turn bad. This was the moment when it became clear to me that I had left my physical body and existed as an astral body *in-between* the *big me* above, and the *sleeping me* below.

Then I felt myself being pulled back into my body, and I woke up from the experience. All of this happened in seconds, while experiencing myself in three different places.

My great soul, the astral me and the little me who was sleeping, coexisted in the same time and dimension. For one brief moment, I became aware of *Self*.

How is that possible? I could swear that I was very conscious at that moment, a little afraid and mesmerized at the same time. I was connected to the bigger me that was observing, and was watching over my astral and physical body. Can it get any more confusing than that?

Besides leaving me more confused, trying to make sense of what just happened, I experienced the presence of that being that had so much love for me, a beautiful, tender, unconditional love, a love that I didn't want to let go.

Days later, my husband and I were talking about the experience. I was desperately trying to make sense of it, when he surprised me by asking if it could be, that in that moment between being asleep and awake I was actually in an astral body, becoming aware of the *bigger me*. Only there I was able to see the big loving being that was me, watching me from above.

One amazing thing for me was that if I was in an astral body I did not feel any different, it was still *me*. However, as powerful and as loving as the bigger *me* was, there was still some part of the current *me* in it.

I felt a love that almost made me cry, it was so pure, so clean, so intense.

I will never forget that experience, because for one moment I found myself in a higher dimension and was able to get a glimpse of the glory of who and what we really are!

MANIFEST OR DE-MANIFEST

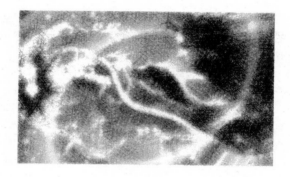

We are energy beings and vibrate at different frequencies. We can alter those frequencies and interact with other energy beings as we choose to.

We are aware of the physical world that we surround ourselves with, but know almost nothing about the non-physical that is constantly around us.

For example, we only need to think of someone in order to interact with that person or situation, *dead or alive*.

However, the scary part is what we unconsciously think of ourselves (again, the *fast food* we have fed our minds in the past and present).

So what we think of us most of the times limit our ability to manifest what we want. What we think of ourselves many time makes us dislike, distrust and betray ourselves in every possible way. If we stop for a moment the way we think of ourselves, what we do and who we think we are, and see ourselves with compassion and love, we'll be able to start reprogramming the mind.

We need the kind of compassion that has no judgment, the compassion that only we can feel for ourselves by accepting that all our wrongs, failures, and bad habits have taught us that we have a choice to change it and transform this experience into neutral wisdom.

That is a precious gift we can always give to ourselves and de-manifest what we don't want out of our experience in life.

THE POWER OF BLESSING

What is the mystery of a blessing? Have you ever thought about how a blessing can influence matter?
A blessing is composed of positive energy and gratitude specifically directed towards something or somebody.

Sometimes a blessing is all that it takes for a situation, a person or an object to perform at its best. If you haven't tried it, I recommend you talk to your body, a specific organ or the mass of trillions of cells that you are, and simply give your gratitude to them for all the hard work they do for you without you even knowing.

It is never too late to be kind to yourself and to appreciate all that you are composed of. When you want a problem to be resolved, give gratitude to the situation and the teachings you have learned from it, then simply tell it to go away and wait a moment. The results will surprise you.
Growing up in poverty, I learned to be grateful for the little and the big things that came into my life.
For example, I used to have a little Ford Focus. By the time I bought this car it was 2 years old and had been patched back together after being involved in an accident. But that didn't bother me, I needed a car and this one was perfect for me and my children because it was within my budget.
From the beginning I treated my car as another member of the family, spoke to it, and told it how much I appreciated it being with me. I gave my car so much appreciation and love, I even changed the oil and the plugs myself. I also transmitted positive thoughts every time I touched my car and it rewarded me by running for many years.
It was even involved in another accident, where it suffered minor damage when it got hit by another car. The car was out of alignment and needed repairs. I fixed it and it continued to run for fourteen years. Then I decided it was time to get another car, and gave it away as a gift to a young girl who needed a vehicle.

As much as she initially appreciated the gift, it still was only an *old car* to her.

Not being granted the same gratitude it was used to, it only survived a few more months before breaking down entirely. The point is that I completely believe that matter responds to the energy of our thoughts. I believe that if I bless the matter regardless of what it is, the matter will react in a positive way and it will last longer and perform harmoniously.

The same has happened to my house and many other things I had during my life. I expressed gratitude many times, gave them a name, talked to them and expressed feelings of love.

I also realized that not only objects feel the effect of appreciation, but situations can be altered by that energy too.

The blessing, when it comes from the heart and has the best intention and appreciation, possesses tremendous power. Most of the time we are not aware of this power; we are not aware of our intentions and our thoughts; we are not aware of what we are and what we create and attract by default. Many times we get lost in confusion but continue to create, unaware of the power that we don't know we possess. Yet, when we see the results or manifestation of how matter or situations react to a blessing, it is a great feeling and a reminder that the universe is responding to us.

For that, if you practice appreciation and sincere gratitude towards everything, your life will transform in front of you.

MEETING WITH THE RAINBOW WOMAN

One Saturday evening, around the time the kids were in their teens and spent a weekend with their father, I went to the casino to have dinner with my boyfriend and his parents.

Afterwards we decided to gamble. It was fun for a minute, but then I got bored. I felt a strong desire to leave and visit Aquarius, a local store I liked to visit for their variety of spiritual things.

I told my boyfriend and his family I was leaving and would see them later.

I went to the store with nothing planned, just the feeling that I needed to be there. Looking around, I heard people talk about the *Rainbow woman* who was there to give a seminar. Apparently, I arrived just in time.

Even though the title of the subject was not necessarily something that I was interested in, I had the feeling that I needed to be there. So I followed my feeling and signed myself in.

The lady introduced herself to a small group of about ten people and told us that she was in contact with her spirit guides, who tell her to go to different places.

She went on mentioning that, during her seminars, she can be talking about something ordinary, while her spirit guides communicate with whomever they need to talk to from the audience. They can be transmitting a message, or helping the person by initiating something within them.

I didn't give it much thought and continued to listen and observe the lady as she was giving her seminar. Suddenly, I physically felt a very strong energy coming from the ground, entering my body through my feet.

This was something I never felt before and I felt a little scared, but also curious of what was happening. Staying still, trying not to move, I felt that energy traveling from my feet all the way to my head. By the time the current of energy traveled all the way to my head, I felt my body warmed, energetic and vibrating differently than usual.

Then I started to feel high energies around me and around that woman.

Only then I finally understood why they called her the Rainbow woman. As she was walking back and forth, talking about something I didn't even pay attention to, I started to see a golden vibrant aura around her, covering her completely. I looked at other people to see if they were experiencing the same phenomenon but they looked normal, and seemed to pay attention to what she was saying.

I thought, it can't only be me who is seeing this, so I raised my hand and told her "I'm sorry to interrupt, but I have to tell you that you have a beautiful golden light around you." She came closer, smiled, and told me, "You are the reason why my spirit guides sent me here." Then, without hesitation, she said, "They must be talking to you right now, because they have a message for you. They're also interacting with your spirit guides."

Before continuing her discussion with the group, she asked me not to leave so we could talk after the seminar.

I was in euphoria, still seeing her shining, while the current of energy was rushing through me. I felt so much joy in my heart, as if I was covered with a warm blanket of light all over me.

Not understanding what was happening but at the same time trying not to panic, I was just going with the flow, seeing where this would take me.

When the session ended. Rainbow woman came and asked me for my name. She told me a little about her life, mentioning that she had a daughter who is even more gifted than she is.

She said her guides had already activated something within me during her visit, while her guides talked to my guides. She asked me if there was anything she could teach me before she left. I said "Yes," she knew how to do soul

regressions, so she did a chart for me.
She also told me that we met before in another life and we worked together towards a common goal.

Later on she mentioned that we met a few thousand years ago, where we shared a common philosophy, but she never told me what role we played or what we accomplished working together. She probably felt my skepticism about the *few thousand years ago* when I raised my eyebrows. She quickly said "In time you will uncover the rest, you must work on that on your own."
The next day she left town.
That experience left me very much in shock with no answers and the feeling that something happened inside me, something I couldn't even explain to myself, something very important, but I didn't know what.

I never again experienced what I had when I met that woman. It was a physical and spiritual phenomenon, a very powerful energy. It felt as if something got awakened, as if a message was given that I received in a very direct way. I felt so much joy and gratitude for her and for the beings that brought her to me, communicated with me, and awoke something from deep inside.

ONE OF THE ELDERS FROM THE GROUP

One day I went to a *church* called Unity looking to hear new theories.

Although I'm free from religion and definitely not a church person, this place is different. They have multiple locations hosting *out of the ordinary* events and speakers.

Once I had a nice experience attending one of their seminars, listening to a speaker talking about tapping the body in order to release emotional issues.

This time I tried a different location and got into one of their groups discussing Buddhism. However, I felt that I was looking for something else. I didn't know what it was, but one Saturday, instead of going to the regular Buddha class, I went in a different direction as if something told me to.

In a smaller area of the building, a group of people gathered together listening to an older man talking. I quietly sat down in one of the chairs close to the door, not knowing what to expect. I thought that this way I could leave if I didn't like it, but became very intrigued about what I was seeing around the man giving the class.

Sometimes I see things around people. Things like energies, spirits, or aura colors. But around this man, I not only saw two bright, very powerful energy beings, but also two additional, less powerful but beautiful spirits. I felt strong emotions hearing this man talk.

The thing is, I had an instant feeling that I knew those energy beings and that man from somewhere out of time. This was a memory that came to me only after seeing them. It was very clear to me that we had met in a different place that wasn't earth, but I couldn't point out where.

In all honesty I did not pay attention to what he was teaching; I was amazed, watching those beings and feeling their energy. It was a feeling of such joy, like when you haven't seen a dear friend in centuries.

I saw how the energy beings were all over the place spreading their peaceful, loving energy. They also brought so much light into the room and around that man that it felt almost overwhelming.

I was fascinated by the feelings I just experienced. I stayed there until the class ended and the man had said his goodbyes to the group. Then he introduced himself as Richard, and welcomed me to the group smiling, while holding my hands. I saw his eyes and I felt a connection with him. I felt joy and my entire body got recharged with the energy of the beings that surrounded him.
I have no idea what he thought of me or if I looked lost in that moment trying to understand what I was experiencing. I didn't tell Richard what was happening to me, because I didn't want to scare him, or for him to tell me that I was in the wrong class.
I went home and reviewed all that happened that morning in my mind. I felt that once again something bigger had guided me to meet this man. I wondered about my feelings about meeting this man in a place that was not earth, and if it wasn't earth then where was it? Then I closed my eyes and a memory came to me. I saw a group of energy beings that were getting together to continue formulating a plan, some sort of a big mission. I identified Richard as one of those beings, while realizing that I belonged to the group too. I felt this happened long ago, as if he was a very old dear friend from before our time on earth. Little pieces of memory fragments continued to come to me.

One day after class I just couldn't hold back what I was experiencing and waited for him to say good bye to everybody else. I approached him and told him about the beautiful and powerful beings around him. Surprised, he asked me if I could see them. I told him "yes, sometimes I see energy beings around people in your case, those beings

are very obvious to me because of their size and power."
It probably was too late, but I didn't want to say more so he wouldn't look at me as a lunatic or crazy person. As time went by I continued to go to the Saturday meetings and got more familiar with the group. In the beginning, I didn't want to participate in the ongoing conversations. I'm used to going to places to learn and move on without developing roots. But this group was different because of him. I feel peaceful and joyful when I'm around him, but also very energetic. This energy charge can last for several hours. Later on, I told Richard what I experienced the first time we met. I told him about my memory of meeting him before in a different place out of time. I felt as if we were other kinds of beings before we came to earth: Beautiful, powerful, amazing beings of light. I told him he was one of the elders of the group. I do not know what he thought of that, or what he thought of me, but I had to tell him: Somehow it was important to me that he knew.
I also felt that the energy that Richard and I share can be very powerful if combined, powerful in the way of helping others.
Later on, Richard and his beautiful wife Marcene shared a story with me about a lady they met years ago who was very intuitive. She told Richard that she saw two powerful spirits around him. One was a woman and the other a man. I believe she even gave them a description of how they looked. It was very rewarding to Richard to hear this confirmation from me about the existence of those beings. Later, I learned that he conducts spiritual healing for people, which explains to me the energy he transmits and why those beings are around him.

THE COLLECTIVE CONSCIOUS/UNCONSCIOUS

As I mentioned earlier, the mind is an amazing tool. It's a tool that receives and filters information through our six senses. However, since most humans neglect the sixth sense, the information received is limited and/or disturbed. With only five senses, our minds are able to comprehend the intellect but not the whole spectrum of our reality. Again, it is not the mind's fault, but what we have fed it with.

Consciousness is a higher reality the mind is not able to comprehend. This is the most difficult part to explain, because our mind has limited words to describe its meaning.

Consciousness is immeasurable awareness, immeasurable understanding of all intelligence. It involves the feeling of love on a grand scale; consciousness is all of what we are with all of what we are made of.

It is every cell collaborating with each other; it's the quantum energy in conjunction with the macro universes. It was the very first thing before the universes came into existence.

It is energy without form. There are different levels of consciousness, and humanity as a whole is experiencing ascension of consciousness in our evolution.

As humans we can only experience a certain degree of consciousness during our lifetimes. If we study history with all of our setbacks and move forward, we can see that many humans are now experiencing a higher level of consciousness.

Consciousness is an energy that has always been there but we are not always the best receptors.

Not so long ago, we were not as capable at receiving this energy and we had to adapt, learn and grow. More important, we had to learn to open our minds to other possibilities. Even though accepting new possibilities was very difficult for many people, there have always been

pioneers on earth who have come to *stir the waters* with new, and many times unimaginable ideas.
Thanks to the increased receptivity in a few people around the globe, the study of consciousness became more appealing to others.

Consciousness in humanity is inevitable and impossible not to acquire since we all participate with transmitting and receiving data, and attracting or repelling energy.

The collective consciousness is *the big picture*, the matrix; it is the ocean of energy we all participate in, at a conscious or unconscious level. With that said, what affects one, affects the rest.
I believe in *interventions* from higher energy beings. I believe they are constantly helping us by intervening with their energy and thoughts in the collective consciousness. Thanks to that energy, we humans are able to receive their messages, their help or warnings.

Some humans are more receptive to that energy than others. When those who are more attune receive the inspiration, the feeling, or the message, they are also able to bring it to the rest of the world in different forms. Consequently, the entire world benefits from it because of the simple fact that *we are all connected.*

REFLECTION

There is magic all around us! I believe there are mysteries in life, things that can't be explained with logic. I've been wondering, who are those beings I see around people? One of the things I noticed months after I met the Rainbow woman was that I became more sensitive to other energies; I became able to see and feel more beings around people. I noticed that some of those beings are more powerful than others, and that not everybody attracts them. I don't know what the difference is between energy beings and spirit guides, but for example, Rainbow woman and Richard both have those powerful beings with them.

These particular beings have no face or gender, and to my limited understanding they are beyond physical appearance and are nothing but pure and powerful energy.
However, I have also seen beings of different genders attached to people that I believe are spirit guides, and I have seen what you would call *ghosts*.
On some occasions, I have even heard their voices and conversations.
Unfortunately, I also have encountered beings of negative energy. Let me explain. I don't see them with my physical eyes, but with my sixth sense, and their image gets imprinted into my mind. But not only their image gets imprinted, also their energy, their vibrational frequency, and their intention.
It is hard to describe something that defies logic to the human mind.
It's always a joyful encounter every time I meet people with good beings around them. I feel their love and get energetic and happy. On the opposite side, it is very disturbing to my body when I met people with negative energies; my body

feels uneasy and sick.

As I said, experiences like these always leave me with many unanswered questions. The point is, that, during our lifetime, we meet people we have met before, because everybody brings different kinds of energies to the human experience.

I believe in the power of believing. When there's a *believe*, anything is possible but when there's none, it's like a book with empty pages.

Believing something gives power to the matter or subject. I believe our words have power, as long as we believe that they do. If we believe that we don't have influence on something, it is also true. In that way, we are creators of our own destiny. If we change our beliefs, our lives will gradually change with them, as well as the world we surround ourselves with. The word is empty without the desired intention.

When we align the heart with the mind on what we intend to do or what to believe in, we create a point of focus where all our energy is directed. The moment we build up enough of that energy, *things happen.*

What do we want to allow to happen in our lives, is the question.

I see it as if every human is born with a book full of empty pages and it is up to us what we want to write on them.

What is the story we want to create? What choices in life do we make? Do we want to be the victim, the predator, the saint, the sinner, all of them or neither?

Whatever we decide to do with our lives is the biggest decision we'll ever make, because there is no one to blame for what we choose to do, or what we make of ourselves.

The truth is that it is all about the experience we chose to have. With reincarnation after reincarnation, we have had the opportunity to be many different kinds of people, some of them good, some of them not so much.

The power to love and accept ourselves can bring out the best in us. As they say, "words don't teach, only life experience does."

By experiencing life in a certain way, we allow ourselves to understand others because we have lived a similar situation. All the lovers and relationships from our past that we believe *did not work for us*, were actually necessary way-points in our journey. They were exactly what we needed in that moment; they created contrast for us to explore.

All passionate relationships start with a spark that brings happiness to our hearts, and our brains explode with serotonin. Later on as the brain chemicals start to dry out, if there's no other kind of foundation that strengthens the feeling, the love dries out too, and it's over.

However, every experience brings something new, something different, something that stays with us until it is time to move on again.

The only eternal love is the love for oneself. Life is every moment, with all that it has and all that it is. And the only true value to the soul is all the love that we are capable of giving. All the relationships we have in our lives, present and past, are carryovers and part of our own plan that we bring into life. We have chosen specific experiences and people for each incarnation who will bring different components. On the bases of these components we will be inspired or motivated to new creations.

THE VOICE FROM DEEP INSIDE (This is our message to you).

After sharing some of my life experiences with you, I also want to tell you my friend; that no, I'm not here to change anyone's religion, or to create a new one. I'm not here to show you the way or be another false messiah. I'm here to ask you to stop following the wrong idols, stop looking for a guru among the living or the dead and dig deep into your heart to find your own truth.
Start to begin believing in yourself.
I realize there's nothing I need to forgive to anyone, only myself. I owe myself so much, because I have neglected, mistreated, and betrayed myself for so long.

Now I know, that if there's a *God* I need to talk to, it is the *God* inside my heart. If there is a mystery I need to solve, it is the mystery of finding myself for who I really am. If there is a place where I should go to find the peace and love I've always yearned for, that place is deep inside my heart. I'm here to ask you to stop being afraid of whatever it is you are afraid of, and to pay attention to the voice from deep inside.
Start asking your own questions and use your own mind and guidance. Stop following the steps of others and start making your own way.
Have the courage to be truthful to yourself, and accept others the way they are; but most important *accept yourself for who you are.*

Learn and take the teachings of what feels right in your gut, and let go of the rest. Everyone has their own truth, and everyone carries their own star. Have the courage to *come out of the closet* and show your true colors (it has nothing to do with gender).

If you have come to the point in your life of asking yourself *what is your mission on earth*, you must know that you never stopped following that mission.
All the way from the moment of birth until the last breath you take, *you continue to follow that mission, that you yourself set into motion from before you even embarked onto this journey on earth.*

You are exactly where you need to be to experience exactly what you are experiencing.
If there's something different you should do, *life will take you there, even against your own will.*
No one's *mission is more important that the rest*, and again it may-be that your greater achievement of experience will come to you at a later date when you might be 50 or 90 years old. Or maybe you are to live a life learning to trust who you are without the distraction of being acknowledged, instead remaining invisible to the world, following your own star.
Allow your guidance to guide you and learn to trust the voice from your heart. ***There is no small role.***

It is OK to be different, there is no right or wrong, but we all must create our own experiences and write them into the empty pages of our destiny book.
It is up to you, how you want your own story to go.
I'm here to remind you that *all your power is in the now.*
I'm here to remind you that *You are God*, more powerful than what your human mind can ever imagine!

THE LATEST REALIZATION OF WHAT I AM

I enjoy going back into my memories, seeing myself as the child I used to be and the woman I have become.
I'm not the same person that I was at certain times, and experiences have transformed my way of understanding life.
However, there's always a part of me that has never changed, the one element that remains the same: The core of my being.
Figuratively if, before being born, someone had shown me a crystal ball with all the different things I would have to go through and face in life, I would probably have declined the offer and said "thanks, but no thanks."

I would probably be terrified if it was my little mind making that decision; but the decision was made by the aware part of my soul.

One of the greatest realization is the complete acceptance of one-self. Yes we have hurt others in this life and in many others, yes we have been hurt by others over and over, and we will continue to repeat this back and forth until we stop and *call for the light*, that will illuminate our thoughts and bring our hearts to the realization that there is nothing to be forgiven, and nothing to forgive to others, but to accept ourselves with unconditional love and compassion.

I choose to believe that I came here with my conscious awareness of what I really am. I choose to believe that I was eager to come to this place, to experience life through a human body.
Knowing the great potential within me, instead of being afraid, I was eager to be here and manifest my desires.

Knowing that even if I forget who I am, I will always be able to find myself, knowing that I didn't come to earth alone but with a group of guides that are always with me, supporting my experience.
Knowing that the goal was never to find myself if I got lost, but to have the experiences I created on my way back to self! *My way back home.*

WITHOUT CONCLUSION

There is no conclusion.
Once upon a time I was whole, I was complete, I was a high vibration energy being, living in complete awareness of self, but I was willing to change it all for the opportunity to serve and be part of the greatest purpose of all.
While I am here on earth, so many realizations have wakened inside me as I continue to remove resistances and fears, I had built for so long.
I am eager to continue to allow myself to experience the full realization of who I am. I realize that the way I came to earth, the parents I had, the environment I grew up in, and the mistakes I have made along with the happiness and profound realizations, were more than just experience.
They have awakened feelings and an understanding of life that I needed for my own development as a human and a soul.
I realize that I could only achieve this understanding by living under those conditions.
I realize how powerful we can be, when we direct our will in a conscious way to attract exactly what we want to experience.
I realize that I am, and I always will be whole, even while taking a human body from earth.
Even though at this point, my mind might not understand the entire concept of what that means, my heart does, as it continues to open itself to love and self-awareness.

And finally, I realize that love is the greatest power of all!

MEDITATION TO CONNECT WITH SELF

I found out that when I tried to connect with my higher self, many times it was difficult for me to get a clear connection and I didn't know why.
It was like I was only getting little pieces of the connection until I tried something else.
I realized I had to remove things from inside of me in order to make room for a more pure energy to enter.
I needed to get rid of other stuff, the kind that clogs my energy and creates resistance in my body.

So this is what I did.
Start with finding a comfortable position either on the couch or the floor.
Then touch the acupressure point in the middle of your chest to calm yourself and bring you into relaxation.

Place a finger there and press softly while deeply breathing in and out for a few minutes, then voice the following:

1. In this moment and in this time I remove all of my fears and put them outside of me.
2. In this moment and in this time I remove all of my anger and put them outside of me.
3. In this moment and in this time I remove all of my self-pity and put them outside of me.
4. In this moment and in this time I remove all of my judgment and put them outside of me.
5. In this moment and in this time I remove all my resistance and put it outside of me.

Go on and on, on the list of things you want to put aside of you for the moment.
Remember you are not getting rid of the *issues*, and you are not fighting with them either. All you are doing is putting

them aside for the moment and you will get them back when done. This way there is no resistance for those emotions to fight back.

After that, ask your higher-self to fill you up and surround you with white light. Next, ask your higher-self (the great observer) to observe you and to connect with you.

The next thing to do, is to put aside your mind and voice the following. "In this moment and in this time, with love and appreciation, I put aside my precious mind- and open my heart to love"
Now all you have to do is experience the energy that comes to you, and you can feel in your heart.
The energy will flow easier because you have made room for it. From there, as everybody is different, you will experience your individual connection with the great observer or higher-self.

POEMS

I am.

I'm the biggest mystery of my own existence!
I'm the center of my universe!
I'm a creature that is transforming itself and the world
around me, as I continue to engage into realization after
realization!
I'm my greatest fear but also my own salvation!
My identity can only be reveal by the true being of who I
am and no one else.
Supreme source; I'm your child, your precious creation-
and you are my all!

From me, to my Higher-Self.

I am the manifestation of the intention that took place in the heart of my creator.
I am the purest form of what once was a desire.
I exist because of the life given to me by the Intender.
I am connected to the all, the visible and the non-visible, I am part of the all.
I am one with the all, I am the essence of the purest intention of creation.
I am the desire – desiring!
I am the mind – creating!
I am the heart – inspiring!
I am the word – expressing!
I am the spirit – manifesting!
I am one with my desire, where everything is possible.
I am the miracle of expansion- where there are no limits or boundaries.
I am the life of the universe, the manifestation of love in its purest form.
I am who I am! And so are you

So be it!

The illusion of separation.

I looked for you in the philosophies of the century; but couldn't find you there.

I looked for you inside the old church, hoping that if I light a candle I will get a glimpse of you; but couldn't find you there.

I looked for you in the stories of man and the science of the future, hoping to find a miracle that will inspire me to see you; but couldn't find you there.

I prayed and cried for long hours, hoping that if you see me on the ground you would come to my rescue; but couldn't find you there.

I looked for you under the stones of the great park and under my bed during the night; but couldn't find you there.

And while I was searching for you, I helped and old lady cross the street. I held her weak hand while we slowly walked ahead. I felt the air, I felt the sun, I felt present in that moment of time.
When we reached the other side she said to me "stop your search and look no more, for what you are looking for, has never left your side!

When I wasn't aware.

The world continued to turn around on its eternal cycle;
But I wasn't aware of it!

The universe was constantly manifesting in front of my
eyes; But I wasn't aware of it!

My heart was continually beating without rest, waiting for
me to uncover its purest message; But I wasn't aware of it!

My blood was smoothly running through my veins
perpetuating life into my cells; But I wasn't aware of it!

My spirit guides were reflecting light onto my long path to
keep me safe; But I wasn't aware of it!

My soul was patiently waiting for me to wake up into
awareness; But I wasn't aware of it!

But today, there is something different about this day, today
for the first time, I became aware of it!

I cannot promise how tomorrow will be, for tomorrow I
haven't lived yet, but this moment, this moment is all I am
aware of it!

MESSAGE FROM SOURCE.

You have never walked alone in the darkness of your shadows, my presence has always carried you without you knowing or understanding.

Sometimes it is hard for you to hear my voice because your focus is on fear. Sometimes it is hard for you to feel my presence because your heart is suppressed with a shield.

Many times I guided you through a different route to keep you safe. Other times I guided you to take the long path instead, because only there you could find the meaning of your search.

Day and night and in between moments I'm there with you, talking to you through your dreams or through the strangers in the street.

When you look for answers, you are looking for me.
When you allow yourself to love yourself, you open the door to the universe that responds.
When you shine your light with kindness and compassion onto others, in that moment you regroup as oneness with the all.

Don't try to understand what I'm, but try to honor what you are, this is the shortest way to me and the wisest way of living life.

I understand you like no one does, and all I want from you is to trust, trust the voice from your heart!

You are my experience, the source that gives life to my expansion in the universe.
I'm the intelligence, the source of life that created you.

Without me you cannot exist, without you, I could never expand.
Creator of life I am in you, leave the path of doubt and follow me. Trust a little more and you will be able to see what you couldn't before, creator of life I am in you.

and so it is.....

47951794R00072

Made in the USA
Middletown, DE
06 September 2017